GREEK

Colophon

© 2003 Rebo International b.v. Lisse, The Netherlands

www.rebo-publishers.com – info@rebo-publishers.com

This 2nd edition reprinted 2004

Original recipes and photographs: © R&R Publishing Pty. Ltd.

Design, editing, production and layout: Minkowsky Graphics, Enkhuizen, The Netherlands

Translation and adaptation: American Pie, London, UK and Sunnyvale, California, USA

ISBN 90 366 1469 4

GREEK

the best recipes from sunny Greece to your kitchen for

creative cooking

REBO
PUBLISHERS

Foreword

For Greek atmosphere, put a blue-and-white checkered tablecloth on the table. Greek food will be a revelation to you. Start in the summer, with a fresh and delicious, ice-cold yogurt soup. Then serve a variety of appetizers (*mezedes*), beautifully arranged on a large tray, a Greek tradition that dates back thousands of years. Following that, you have a wide choice of meat, fish, and vegetables. The Greeks work magic with everything from Leg of Lamb with Lima Beans, Olives, and Risoni to Psari Plaki (Fried Fish) and Artichokes La Polita. This book shows you the traditional Greek ways of cooking meats, vegetables, and herbs. As the grand finale, spoil yourself with a dessert drenched with honey from Mount Hymettus, and the Greek myth is complete.

Abbreviations

tbsp = tablespoon

tsp = teaspoon

g = gram

kg = kilogram

fl oz = fluid ounce

lb = pound

oz = ounce

ml = milliliter

l = liter

°C = degree Celsius

°F = degree Fahrenheit

Where three measurements are given,

the first is the American liquid measure.

Method

1. Place all ingredients for the salad in a bowl.

2. Combine olive oil and vinegar in a bowl, and beat with a whisk. Pour this over the salad, then season with salt and ground black pepper.

3. Serve salad on its own, or with fresh bread. Garnish with oregano leaves.

Greek salad

Ingredients

2 small cucumbers, sliced

4 beefsteak tomatoes, quartered

2 Bermuda onions, sliced or quartered

5 tbsp/2½ oz/80 g feta cheese, crumbled

½ cup/4oz/125g Kalamata olives, left whole

3 tbsp/45ml olive oil

2 tbsp/30g brown vinegar

salt

freshly ground black pepper

oregano leaves, for garnish

greek

Method

1. Pre-heat the broiler. Place the bell pepper quarters under the broiler and broil until it turns black on top. Cut into strips, scrape out the ribs, and set aside.

2. In a small jar, combine all ingredients for dressing, and shake well.

3. In a frying pan, heat 1 tbsp/15ml olive oil. Add the walnuts and cook for 1-2 minutes or until lightly browned. Toss the salad in a large salad bowl, drizzle with the dressing, and serve with pita bread.

Ingredients

1 red bell pepper, quartered and seeded

4 tsp/20ml olive oil

3½oz/100g walnuts

7oz/200g baby spinach, washed

7oz/200g feta cheese, cubed

10oz/300g artichoke hearts, quartered

½ cup/4oz/125g black olives, pitted

pita bread, for serving

Baby spinach, feta, artichoke, and walnut salad

Dressing:

½ cup/4fl oz/125ml extra virgin olive oil

4 tbsp/65ml/2fl oz lemon juice

2 tsp/10ml honey

2 tsp/10ml oregano (chopped)

pepper (freshly ground)

Method

1. Soak chickpeas in cold water overnight. Place chickpeas in a saucepan covered with water and bring to the boil, then simmer for around one hour or until chick peas are cooked. Drain and set aside.

2. Pre-heat the oven to 400°F/200°C. Halve the tomatoes and place them in a roasting pan. Cut the top off the garlic bulb and place in the roasting pan.

3. Drizzle with olive oil, sprinkle with salt and dried oregano, and bake in the oven for 20-30 minutes.

4. Place the tomatoes and five peeled garlic cloves (reserve the rest) in a food processor, and purée for one minute.

5. Heat half the oil and sauté the leeks for three minutes. Add the broth, and bring to the boil, then reduce heat to simmer.

6. Add the tomato mixture, tomato paste, and the chickpeas, season with salt and pepper, and heat through.

7. To serve, sprinkle with fresh oregano leaves just before serving.

Ingredients

4 cups/1lb/500g dried chickpeas

8 cups/2lb/1kg beefsteak tomatoes

1 bulb garlic

5 tbsp/2½oz /85ml olive oil

salt

Chickpea, roasted tomato, and garlic
soup

2 tbsp/30ml dried oregano

2 leeks, sliced, white part only

1 quart/1¾ pints/1 l chicken broth

2 tbsp/30ml tomato paste

salt and pepper

fresh oregano leaves

Tzatziki (Cucumber with yogurt and mint)

1. Combine all the ingredients in a bowl, and season with salt and pepper to taste. Cover with plastic wrap and refrigerate for at least one hour to allow the flavors to develop).

2. Serve with pita bread as a dip, or as an appetizer.
   Makes 1 cup/8 fl oz/250ml.

Roasted eggplant and garlic dip

1. Pre-heat the oven to 400°F/200°C.

2. Place the eggplant and garlic in a roasting pan, drizzle with olive oil, and bake in the oven for 20 minutes. Remove from the oven, scoop the flesh out of the inside of the eggplant, and place the flesh and roasted garlic in the bowl of a food processor.

3. Process until smooth, then add the tahini, lemon juice, and olive oil, and process for a few seconds to combine.

4. Season to taste with salt and pepper, and serve with pita bread.
   Makes 2 cups/16 fl oz/500ml.

Taramosalata (Fish roe salad)

1. Remove crusts from bread and soak the bread in water for ten minutes Squeeze bread dry, and place in food processor. Process for one minute.
   Add the taramosalata, and process for another minute.

2. With the processor still running, pour the oil in a continuous stream until all the oil has been added and the mixture is creamy and thick.

3. Add the juice of the lemon, and the water, and process until well combined. Remove, place in a bowl, and store in the refrigerator for up to seven days.

4. Serve with toasted pita bread.
   Makes approximately 2½ cups/1 pint/600ml.

Dips

Tzatziki (Cucumber with yogurt and mint)

¾ cup/6oz/185g plain Greek yogurt
⅓ cup/3oz/90g grated cucumber
1 tbsp/15ml lemon juice
1 clove garlic, crushed
salt and black pepper
1 tbsp/15ml chopped mint (optional)

Roasted eggplant and garlic dip

1 large eggplant (aubergine)
5 cloves garlic, roasted

1 tbsp/15ml tahini
1 tbsp/15ml lemon juice
1 tbsp/15ml olive oil
salt and black pepper

Taramosalata (Fish roe salad)

4 slices day-old white bread
⅓ cup/3oz/90g jar pink cod or salmon roe
¾ cup/6fl oz/185ml vegetable oil
¾ cup/6fl oz/185ml olive oil
1 lemon juice squeezed
1 tbsp/15ml water

Method

1. Pre-heat oven to 350°F/180°C.

2. Cut the tops off each tomato, and scoop the centers into a bowl. Dice the tops, and add to the bowl. Combine half the tomato mixture with the feta, ricotta, pine nuts, olives, oregano, bread crumbs, and pepper. Beat mixture together, and spoon back into the cases, piling the tops high.

3. Place in a shallow oven-proof dish and bake for 20-25 minutes.

4. Garnish with an olive and oregano to serve.

Feta and ricotta stuffed **tomatoes**

Ingredients

6 large firm tomatoes

⅔ cup/5oz/150g feta cheese, crumbed

⅔ cup/5oz/150g ricotta cheese

4 tbsp/2oz/60g pine nuts, chopped

10 black olives, pitted and chopped

1½ tbsp/20g fresh oregano, chopped

3 tbsp/45g whole-wheat bread crumbs

freshly ground black pepper

6 black olives, to garnish

oregano leaves

Method

1. Peel and grate the cucumber.

2. Combine the cream, yogurt, and vinegars together, and whisk lightly, until smooth. Stir in the cucumber, mint, garlic, and seasoning. Cover and chill for three hours.

3. Stir and taste for seasoning before serving chilled. Garnish with a slice of cucumber, a sprig of mint and cracked pepper.

Ingredients

1 long cucumber

1 cup/8 oz/250ml light (single) cream

1 scant cup/7fl oz/200ml natural yogurt

2 tbsp/30g white wine vinegar

1 tbsp/15 ml balsamic vinegar

2 tbsp/30g fresh mint, chopped

Chilled yogurt **soup**

1 clove garlic, crushed

salt and freshly ground black pepper

extra mint and slices of cucumber, to garnish.

Method

1. Place the cheese on a plate. Combine together the garlic, thyme, lemon, pepper, and oil. Spoon this over the cheese. Cover and place in fridge to marinate for 4-6 hours.

2. Pre-heat the broiler. Broil the cheese for 3-4 minutes on each side. Broil the lemon until softened.

3. Arrange salad leaves on four plates. Place a piece of cheese on each, with a little lemon, and drizzle some of the marinade oil over the cheese.

4. Serve with warm toast or toasted pita bread.

Broiled goat's cheese **salad**

Ingredients

4 small fresh goat's cheeses

1 clove garlic, crushed

1 sprig thyme, chopped

½ lemon, halved and thinly sliced

cracked pepper

5 tbsp/2½fl oz/80ml extra virgin olive oil

2½ cups/10oz/300g mixed salad leaves

toasted bread

Method

Cook the orzo in a large pot of boiling salted water until tender but al dente. Drain and rinse under cold water then place in a large bowl with a little olive oil from the dressing ingredients.

Add the crumbled feta cheese, chopped peppers, Kalamata olives, green onions, and capers.

To make the dressing, whisk together the lemon juice and zest, vinegar, garlic, oregano, mustard, and cumin in a small bowl. Gradually add the remaining olive oil, then season to taste with salt and pepper.

Drizzle the dressing over the salad and toss thoroughly then garnish with the toasted pine nuts.

Ingredients

1½ cups/12oz/350g orzo or rice-shaped pasta

¾ cup/6oz/170g feta cheese, crumbled

1 red bell pepper, finely chopped

1 yellow bell pepper, finely chopped

1 green bell pepper, finely chopped

¾ cup/6½ oz/180g pitted Kalamata olives, chopped

4 green onions (scallions), sliced

2 tbsp/30g drained capers

Greek orzo salad
with olives and bell peppers

Dressing:

2 lemons, rind and juice

1 tbsp/15g white wine vinegar

1 tbsp/15g minced garlic

1½ tsp/7.5g dried oregano

1 tsp/5g Dijon mustard

1 tsp/5g ground cumin

⅓ cup/3½ oz/100ml olive oil

3 tbsp/45g pine nuts, toasted

greek

Method

1. Combine the ground beef, onions, parsley, rice, and egg in a bowl, and mix well with your hands. Season well with salt and pepper. Using 1 tbsp/15g of mixture for each meatball, shape mixture into balls, and roll in cornstarch, shaking off the excess).

2. Bring the broth and the butter to the boil, then reduce the heat and place the meatballs in the broth. Cover with a lid, and simmer for 45 minutes (until they are cooked). Let cool slightly.

3. Whisk the egg and lemon juice together in a bowl, then add 100ml/3fl oz of warm broth to the egg and lemon juice. Pour this mixture back into the saucepan and heat very gently.

4. Season with salt and pepper before serving.

Meatballs in egg and lemon soup (Youvarlakia)

Ingredients

2 cups/1lb/450g lean ground beef

1 medium onion, minced

¼ cup/2oz/50g parsley, chopped

¼ cup/2oz/50g short-grain rice

1 egg

salt and pepper

⅓ cup/1½ tbsp/20g cornstarch

4cups/1¾ pints/1 l beef broth

3 tbsp/1½oz/50g butter

1 egg

4½ tbsp/2¼fl oz/75ml lemon juice

Method

1. Drain the haricot beans and chickpeas. Place in a saucepan, cover with water, and bring to the boil for 15 minutes. Cover and simmer for a further 30 minutes before draining again.

2. Heat the oil in a saucepan and add the onion, garlic, and leek. Continue stirring until tender. Add the broth, haricot beans, and chickpeas. Cover, and simmer for 45 minutes (until tender). Add the remaining ingredients and simmer for a further 15 minutes.

3. Taste for seasoning, and serve with freshly grated Parmesan.

Mixed bean and vegetable **soup**

Ingredients

½ cup/4oz/125g haricot beans, soaked overnight

½ cup/4oz/125g chickpeas, soaked overnight

3 tbsp/45ml olive oil

1 medium onion, diced

1 clove garlic, crushed

1 leek, white part only; diced

6 cups/2½ pints/1½ l vegetable broth

2 sticks celery, sliced

1 carrot, diced

2 sprigs fresh thyme, chopped

1 small fennel bulb, grated

2 zucchini (courgettes), grated

⅓ cup/3oz/90g lima (broad) beans

3 medium tomatoes, peeled, seeded and chopped

salt and freshly ground black pepper

freshly grated Parmesan, for serving.

Method

1. Brush four sheets of aluminum foil with olive oil. Divide fillets into four servings and arrange flat in center of each foil, skin side down.

2. Pre-heat oven to 350°F/180°C.

3. Combine (in a bowl) the tomato, green pepper, capers, fennel, tomato paste, garlic, lemon juice, salt and freshly ground black pepper. Mix well, and spoon this over the fillets. Dot with a little butter on the tops, and seal the foil over the fish.

4. Bake in a roasting pan for 17 minutes. (Open one package to check the sardines are cooked.) Garnish with lemon wedges. Serve with a fresh salad.

(Psari Plaki)

Ingredients

1 tsp/5ml olive oil

6oz/185g (small can) sardine fillets

2 tomatoes, peeled and diced

½ green bell pepper, seeded and finely diced

1 tsp/5g capers, finely chopped

1 tsp/5g fennel, finely chopped

Baked sardine **fillets**

2 tsp/10ml tomato paste

1 clove garlic, crushed

1⅓fl oz/40ml lemon juice

salt and freshly ground black pepper

1 tbsp/½ oz/15g butter

lemon wedges (to garnish)

Method

1. Lightly brush broiler pan with oil, and heat. Lightly brush sardines with oil, then add to pan and cook for 1-2 minutes each side.

2. Set aside on a plate, and pour 1 tbsp/15ml lemon juice over sardines.

3. Combine the olive oil, extra lemon juice, oregano, pepper, and salt. Mix until well combined. On a plate (or bowl) add spinach or rocket, add slices of red pepper, place four sardines on top, and drizzle dressing over sardines.

Ingredients

1-2 tbsp/15-30ml olive oil

8oz/250g sardine fillets (16 sardines)

1 tbsp/15ml lemon juice

2fl oz/60ml virgin olive oil, extra

1½fl oz/40ml lemon juice, extra

1 tbsp/15g oregano, chopped

Sardines & broiled peppers

freshly ground pepper and salt

2 red peppers, roasted and thinly sliced

2 cups/7oz/200g baby spinach or rocket,

washed and trimmed

greek

greek

Method

1. Prepare artichoke hearts. Strip away outer leaves and trim around base.
    Cut off top ⅓ of artichoke, scoop out center. Cut in half. Place in a bowl of cold
    water with a squeeze of lemon juice (to prevent discoloring).

2. Heat half the oil in a large saucepan. Add shallots and dill, sauté until soft.

3. Cross cut root end of onions, and place in saucepan. Arrange carrots and pota-
    toes. Add lemon juice, remaining oil, salt and pepper (and enough water to
    cover), then cook for 15 minutes.

4. Place artichoke hearts over vegetables and cook for 15 minutes more (or until
    tender).

5. With a slotted spoon, remove vegetables to a heated platter.
    Arrange attractively, displaying the various vegetables. Keep warm.

6. Taste cooking liquid, and add salt, pepper, and lemon juice, and adjust
    (if necessary). Stir in blended arrowroot, and stir over heat to thicken sauce.
    Spoon over vegetables. Serve hot with crusty bread as
    a main course

Artichokes la polita

Ingredients

6 globe artichoke hearts

½ cup/4fl oz/125ml olive oil

½ cup/4oz/125g shallots, chopped

2 tbsp/30g fresh dill, chopped

3 cups/1lb/450g baby carrots, peeled

12 pickling onions, peeled

12 small new potatoes

juice of 1 lemon

water

salt, pepper

2 tbsp/30g arrowroot, blended

Method

1. Pre-heat oven to 350°F/180°C.

2. Heat 1 tbsp/15ml oil in a large frying pan, add leek and garlic, and cook for five minutes or until soft. Set aside.

3. Heat extra oil, add chicken in batches, and cook for 6-8 minutes.

4. Drain spinach, squeeze out excess water, and chop roughly.

5. In a large bowl, combine chicken, spinach, bell pepper, olives, feta, parsley, oregano, eggs, cream and pepper. Stir until well combined. Set aside.

6. Lightly grease a 9 in/22cm square baking pan. Combine the extra oil and butter. Lay out sheets of filo, put two together, and brush with the oil mixture. Put another two on top, and brush again. Continue until you have four double sheets. Line the baking dish with the filo, and trim around the edges. Fill with the chicken mixture. Brush the remaining sheets with oil in the same way as before, using the same amount. Place the filo on top of the baking dish, tucking the edges inside baking dish.

7. Brush the top with the oil mixture, sprinkle with sesame seeds, and bake in the oven for 40-45 minutes.

Ingredients

2 tbsp/30ml olive oil

1 large leek, washed and sliced

1 clove garlic, crushed

1lb/500g chicken breasts, diced

1 bunch spinach, washed and blanched

2 red bell peppers, roasted and diced

3 tbsp/1½oz/40g black olives, pitted and halved

¾ cup/6oz/200g feta cheese, crumbled

Chicken, roasted bell pepper, olive &
feta pie

2 tbsp/30g parsley, chopped

1 tbsp/15g oregano, chopped

3 eggs

¼ cup/2 fl oz/60ml heavy cream

freshly ground pepper

8-16 sheets filo dough

1 tbsp/15ml olive oil, extra

1 tbsp/½oz/15g butter, melted

1 tbsp sesame seeds

Method

1. Pre-heat oven, to 350°F/180°C.

2. In a large heavy-based ovenproof dish heat 1 tbsp/15ml olive oil, add meat and sear quickly on all sides. Take out and set aside.

3. Heat extra olive oil, add garlic and onions, and cook for 2-3 minutes. Add white wine, cook for one minute, then add beef broth, tomato paste, oregano, and salt and pepper. Bring to boil, return meat to dish, add artichokes, cover, and bake for 30-40 minutes.

4. Add olives in the last five minutes of cooking time.

5. Slice the meat and arrange with vegetables; pour the sauce over meat and vegetables.

* Trim artichokes of outer leaves and stems. Place in a bowl of water with lemon juice. This stops the artichokes from turning brown.

Beef with artichokes, olives and oregano

Ingredients

2 tbsp/30ml olive oil

1½lb/750g fillet steak

1 clove garlic, crushed

1 bunch spring onions, trimmed and halved

½ cup/4fl oz/125ml dry white wine

1 cup/8fl oz/250ml beef broth

1 tbsp/15ml tomato paste

2 tsp/10g oregano, chopped

salt and freshly ground pepper

2 globe artichokes, trimmed, and cut into quarters*

⅓ cup/2½oz/100g olives, pitted

Method

1. Pre-heat oven to 350°F/180°C.

2. Place bell peppers in a roasting pan. Place eggplant (aubergine) slices, tomatoes, olives and feta inside bell peppers. In a jar, mix together olive oil, oregano, and garlic. Drizzle this oil mixture over bell peppers, and bake for 20-25 minutes.

Roasted red bell peppers with feta, eggplant, olives, & sun-dried tomatoes

Ingredients

2 large red bell peppers, halved and seeded

2 baby eggplant (aubergine), sliced

¼ cup/60g/2oz semi sun-dried tomatoes

3 tbsp/50g/1½oz olives

⅓ cup/100g/3oz Greek feta, cubed

2 tbsp/20ml olive oil

2 tsp/10g oregano

1 clove garlic, crushed

Method

1. Prepare fish, leaving head and tail on. Make diagonal cuts on surface, sprinkle with a little salt and pepper and lemon juice. Set aside for 20 minutes.

2. Heat half the oil in a frying pan, and sauté onion, garlic, and celery for three minutes. Add tomatoes, wine and oregano, and season with salt and pepper. Sauté a further two minutes.

3. Pre-heat the oven to 350°F/180°C, Spread mixture in an oiled roasting pan and place fish on top. Drizzle remaining oil over fish. Bake for 30-40 minutes, depending on size. Baste fish during cooking.

4. Remove fish to serving platter, spoon sauce around fish, and serve with vegetable accompaniments or a salad.

Baked fish (Psari Plaki)

Ingredients

3lb/1½kg whole snapper or bream

salt and pepper

1 lemon. juice squeezed

½ cup/4fl oz/125ml olive oil

1 large onion, sliced

3 cloves garlic, thinly sliced

½ cup/4oz/125g celery, chopped

1¾ cups/13oz/425g can tomato pieces, peeled

½ cup/4fl oz/125ml dry white wine, optional

½ tsp/2.5g sugar

1 tsp/5g oregano

Method

1. In a bowl, mix together the olive oil, lemon rind and juice, shallots, oregano, and pepper, and salt. Add the octopus, and leave to marinate for one hour.

2. Heat a broiler pan, lightly brush with oil, add octopus, and broil, basting with marinade, for 2-3 minutes, or until tender.

3. Serve on a bed of salad leaves.

Ingredients

⅓ cup/2½ fl oz/80ml olive oil

1 lemon, rind grated

2 tbsp/30ml lemon juice

⅓ cup/3½oz/100g shallots, finely sliced

2 tsp/10g oregano, chopped

Baby octopus marinated in olive oil & oregano

freshly ground pepper and salt

1½ lb/750g baby octopus, cleaned

salad leaves, for serving

Method

Pat salmon dry with a kitchen towel to remove excess liquid.

Combine (in a bowl) the salmon, feta, green onions, sun-dried tomatoes, lemon rind, capers, salt, and freshly ground black pepper.

Cut the filo sheets in half, and cover with a lightly damp cloth.

Pre-heat oven to 400°F/200°C.

Brush four sheets with butter and place on top of each other. Cut into four strips. Repeat with the remaining ingredients.

Divide mixture into four, place spoonfuls of mixture on dough, and roll up to form a package.

Brush packages with butter, and place on a nonstick cookie sheet.

Bake for 10-12 minutes until crisp and golden, and serve warm. Serve with Lemon Yogurt.

To make the Lemon Yogurt, combine all ingredients in a small bowl.

Salmon and feta filo **packages**

Ingredients

⅔ cup/5oz/150g poached salmon, flaked

⅔ cup/5oz/150g feta cheese, crumbled

2 green onions (scallions), finely sliced

2 tbsp/1oz/30g sun-dried tomatoes, finely sliced

1 lemon, rind grated

1 tbsp/15g capers, finely chopped

salt and freshly ground black pepper

6 sheets filo pastry (16 x 12 in/40 x 30cm)

¼ cup/2oz/30g melted butter

Lemon Yogurt

1 scant cup/7oz/200g yogurt

1 tbsp/15g chives, finely sliced

2 tbsp/30ml lemon juice

salt and pepper (to taste)

Method

1. Remove the stalks from eggplant (aubergine) and slice them lengthwise thinly 5mm/2in.Brush the slices on both sides with oil, and broil on both sides (until soft and beginning to brown).

2. Pre-heat the oven to 350°F/180°C. Combine together (in a bowl) the tomatoes, mozzarella, basil, and seasoning. Spoon a little onto the end of each slice of eggplant (aubergine), and roll up. Place seam-side down in a greased ovenproof dish, bake for 15-17 minutes.

3. In a small frying pan, heat a little of the dressing oil, sauté the tomato until softened. Add the remaining oil, balsamic vinegar, and pine nuts, and gently warm. Season to taste. Arrange the rolls on a platter, and spoon the dressing over the rolls.

4. Garnish with fresh basil leaves to serve.

Ingredients

2 x 7oz/225g eggplant (aubergines)

3 tbsp/45ml olive oil

3 medium tomatoes, seeded and diced

5oz/150g mozzarella cheese, finely diced

2 tbsp/30g fresh basil, chopped

salt and freshly ground black pepper

Eggplant **rolls**

fresh basil leaves, for serving

Dressing:

½fl oz/60ml olive oil

1 tbsp/15ml balsamic vinegar

1 tomato, diced

2 tbsp/30g pine nuts, toasted

greek

Method

1. Slice haloumi cheese very thinly, then brush with olive oil, and broil under a broiler until starting to brown.

2. Place the lima (broad) beans and haloumi in a bowl, and add the lemon juice, olive oil, salt and ground black pepper, and serve. Serve with toasted pita bread.

Note:

If the beans are too large, peel off outer skin.

Lima beans with broiled haloumi and lemon

Ingredients

3oz/100g haloumi cheese, halved

oil for brushing

½ cup/8oz/250g broad beans*, fresh or frozen

5 tbsp/2½fl/65ml oz lemon juice

4 tbsp/2fl oz/80ml olive oil

salt and ground black pepper

4 rounds pita bread

Method

1. Combine the eggs and oregano in a bowl, and season with black pepper. Set aside.

2. Heat the oil in a 9in/22cm pan and sauté the potato, onion and garlic for a few minutes until soft.

3. Add the spinach and cook until spinach begins to wilt. Remove the pan from the heat, then add olives, feta, and semi-dried tomatoes.

4. Return the pan to a very low heat, pour in the egg mixture, and cook for 10-15 minutes. Run a spatula around the sides of the pan as the frittata is cooking, and tilt it slightly whilst cooking, so that egg mixture runs down the sides a little.

5. When frittata is almost done through the middle, place under a broiler for five minutes to cook and brown the top.

6. Serve in wedges with the roasted bell pepper sauce.

7. To make the sauce, halve the bell peppers and remove the seeds. Broil the bell peppers until black. Let them cool, and remove the skins. Place into a food processor and process until puréed. Transfer to a bowl.

   Makes 1 cup/8fl oz`/250ml.

Ingredients

10 eggs

1 tbsp/15g oregano, fresh, chopped

black pepper, freshly crushed

5tbsp/2½fl oz/65ml olive oil

1 scant cup/7oz/200g potatoes, peeled and diced

1 brown onion, diced

Spinach, olive and feta frittata with roasted bell pepper sauce

1 clove garlic, crushed

1⅓ cups/5oz/150g baby spinach

2 tbsp/2oz/60g pitted Kalamata olives, halved

5 tbsp/2½oz/80g feta, crumbled

¼ cup/2oz/60g semi-dried tomatoes

3 large red bell peppers

Method

1. Wash chicken livers and remove any sinews. Chop livers into bite-sized pieces.

2. Heat butter in a large saucepan and sauté the shallots for 5 minutes or until tender.

3. Add the chicken livers, and cook for a further few minutes, until they change color.

4. Add the rice and chicken broth to the saucepan, bring to the boil, then simmer (with the lid on), stirring occasionally, for approximately 30 minutes, or until the liquid has been absorbed and the rice is cooked.

    If the rice is not cooked and the mixture is looking a little dry add 1 cup/8 fl oz/250ml of water, and cook for a further five minutes.

5. When rice is cooked, toss the chopped parsley, pinenuts, and currants through the rice, and serve.

Ingredients

5 cups/2½lb/1kg chicken livers

5 tbsp/2½oz/75g butter

12 shallots, chopped

1½ cups/12oz/375g short grain rice

2½ cups/1 pint/600ml chicken stock

½ cup/125g parsley, chopped

⅓ cup/3oz/100g pine nuts

⅓ cup/3oz/100g currants

Rice with chicken livers, pine nuts, and currants

Method

1. Rinse out the Cornish hens (poussins), and pat dry. Combine together the honey, oil, juice, thyme and wine. Place the Cornish hens (poussins) in a bowl and pour half liquid over them. Cover and refrigerate over night. Turn poultry over once or twice during the marinating time.

2. Pre-heat the oven to 350°F/180°C.

3. Wrap the Cornish hens (poussins) in grape leaves and secure with skewers. Bake in a roasting pan for 25-30 minutes. Remove leaves, and return the Cornish hens (poussins) to the oven for 10 minutes, or until cooked through and brown.

4. Remove the skewers, and place the Cornish hens (poussins) on the grape leaves.

5. Heat remainder of marinade in pan, and pour it over the Cornish hens (poussins) before serving.

Cornish hens (poussin) in grape leaves

Ingredients

2 Cornish hens (poussins), halved

4 tbsp/40ml liquid honey

4 tbsp/40ml olive oil

4 tbsp/40ml orange juice

2 tsp/10g lemon thyme, finely chopped

½ cup/4fl oz/125ml white wine

8-10 fresh or marinated grape leaves

Tip

Soften fresh grape leaves by pouring boiling water over them and marinating them in vinegar and olive oil before use. Preserved grape leaves can be used out of season.

Method

1. Grind the almonds in a food processor with a little of the sugar. Combine the remaining sugar with the eggs, and whisk until pale and creamy. Add the ground almonds to the bread crumbs, and stir until well combined.

2. Pre-heat oven to 350°F/180°C.

3. Use a tablespoon to make the mixture into diamond shapes, and place on a non-stick cookie sheet. Bake for 15 minutes.

4. While still warm, place on wire cooling racks, and brush with warm honey. Leave to cool a little before serving.

Ingredients

4 cups/1lb/500g almonds, blanched

1 cup/8oz/250g superfine (caster) sugar

2 medium eggs

4 tbsp/20g soft white bread crumbs

5 tbsp/80ml liquid honey

Almond cakes (kourebides)

Method

1. Season chicken with dried oregano, pepper and salt.

2. Heat oil in a large frying pan.

3. Add chicken, potatoes, and onions, and brown quickly for 2-3 minutes.

4. Pour in broth, cover, and simmer for 10-15 minutes, or until chicken is cooked.

5. Add lemon juice and fresh oregano. Cook for a further three minutes. Serve immediately.

Chicken with oregano and lemon

Ingredients

4 chicken breasts

2 tsp/10g oregano, dried

freshly ground pepper and salt

2 tbsp/30ml olive oil

1½ lb/600g potatoes, cut into ¼ in/5mm slices

1 bunch green onions (scallions), trimmed and halved

½ cup/4fl oz/125ml chicken broth

¼ cup/2½ fl oz/75ml lemon juice

2 sprigs oregano, chopped

salt and pepper to taste

Method

1. Soak wooden skewers in cold water for 30 minutes.

2. In a bowl, combine the yogurt, garlic, paprika, cumin seeds, lemon juice, parsley, oregano, and pepper.

3. Arrange chicken on wooden skewers and brush with half the mixture. Leave to marinate in refrigerator for 2-3 hours.

4. Heat oil on barbecue grill or in broiler pan, add chicken kabobs and cook 4-5 minutes each side.

5. Serve with remaining marinade mixture.

Ingredients

6 chicken thigh fillets, cubed

1¼ cups/10fl oz/300g plain yogurt

2 clove garlic, crushed

1½ tsp paprika, ground

1½ tsp cumin seeds

2fl oz/60ml lemon juice

Chicken kebabs with yogurt and lemon sauce

2 tbsp/30g chopped parsley

2 tsp/10g chopped oregano

freshly ground pepper

24 wooden skewers

greek

Method

1. Sift the flour into a bowl and make a well in the center. Pour the egg yolk, olive oil, and cold water into the well. Whisk the center, gradually incorporating the flour, until a smooth batter has formed. Season with salt and pepper, cover, and leave to thicken for 30 minutes in a cool place.

2. Grate the fennel and zucchini. Stir them into the batter with the mint. Whisk the egg-white until soft peaks form, and fold gently into the batter mixture.

3. Shallow fry spoonfuls of mixture, a few at a time. Cook until golden on both sides and cooked in the center. Drain on paper towels.

4. Serve warm with garlic-flavored plain yogurt.

Fennel & zucchini **cakes**

Ingredients

1⅓ cups/6oz/175g all-purpose (plain) flour

1 egg, separated

1 tbsp olive oil

2½fl oz/75ml cold water

¼ tsp/1.25g each salt and freshly ground black pepper

½ cup/4oz/250g fennel bulb

1 cup/8oz/250g zucchini (courgette)

1 tbsp/15g mint, chopped

oil for shallow frying

garlic-flavored plain yogurt

Method

1. Heat oil in a large saucepan. Add garlic, lamb shanks, and onion, and cook for five minutes, or until shanks are lightly browned.

2. Add the beef broth, sprigs of oregano, tomato paste, and half the water. Bring to the boil, reduce the heat, cover, and leave to simmer for 40 minutes.

3. Remove shanks, slice meat off bone, and set aside.

4. Add the risoni and water, cook for a further five minutes, then add lima (broad) beans, olives, meat, oregano, and salt and pepper, cook for five minutes more, and serve.

Note:

If lima (broad) beans are large, peel off outer skin.

Ingredients

2 tbsp/30ml olive oil

2 cloves garlic, crushed

4 lamb shanks

1 onion, minced

2 cups/16fl oz/450ml beef broth

4 sprigs oregano

2 tbsp/20ml tomato paste

Lamb shanks with lima (broad) beans, olives & risoni

2 cups/16fl oz/500ml water

1 cup/8oz/250g risoni (rice)

1 cup/8oz/250g lima (broad) beans*

½ cup/4 oz/125g olives

2 tsp/10g fresh oregano, chopped

salt and freshly ground pepper

greek

Method

1. Trim and wash zucchini (courgettes) before steaming in a colander for 12-15 minutes (until tender). Press out any excess moisture with the back of a wooden spoon.

2. Finely chop the zucchini, and place in a large mixing bowl. Pre-heat oven to 350°F/180°C, and grease a 8 x 9in/20-24cm pie pan with butter.

3. Soak the feta in warm water for ten minutes and, drain. Mash cheese into a paste, and add to zucchini (courgettes). Combine with the remaining ingredients, and stir well.

4. Pour into the prepared pie pan, sprinkle with a little extra Parmesan, bake for 45 minutes (or until set). Test the center with a skewer before serving.

Zucchini and feta **pie**

Ingredients

5 cups/1½lb/750g zucchini (courgettes)

1 cup/8oz/250g feta cheese

4 eggs, beaten

2 tbsp/30g toasted walnuts, chopped

2 tbsp/30g fresh dill, finely chopped

2 tbsp/30g fresh flat-leaved parsley, minced

¼ cup/2oz/50g Parmesan, freshly grated

black pepper, freshly ground

1 tbsp/15g Parmesan, grated, plus extra for serving

Method

1. Wash and trim okra. In a large bowl, whisk the egg until frothy, add flour and water, and whisk together until the batter is frothy.

2. Heat the oil in a large frying pan, dip okra in batter, and cook in oil for 1-2 minutes or until lightly browned.

3. Drain on absorbent paper and serve with lemon wedges and the sauce.

Method

1. In a small bowl, soak bread in water for five minutes, squeeze out water.

2. Place walnuts in a food processor, and process until finely chopped. Add bread, garlic, and white wine vinegar, and process until combined. While motor is running, add olive oil, and salt and pepper, process until paste is formed. Serve with chicken, fish, or vegetables.

Garlic walnut sauce
Ingredients

2 slices day-old bread

⅔ cup/5fl oz/150ml water

¼ cup/2oz/60g walnuts

2 cloves garlic, roughly chopped

2 tbsp/1fl oz/30ml white wine vinegar

4 tsp/20ml olive oil

salt and pepper, to taste

Ingredients

2 cups/8oz/250g okra

1 cup/4oz/125g all-purpose flour

1 egg

1 cup/8fl oz/250ml ice water

oil for frying

Deep-fried okra

For the garlic-walnut sauce

2 slices day-old bread

¾ cup/6fl oz/170ml water

¼ cup/2oz/60g walnuts

2 garlic cloves, coarsely chopped

2 tbsp/30 ml white wine vinegar, 4 tsp/20 ml olive oil

pepper and salt to taste

greek

Method

1. In a bowl, combine the chopped onion, mince, bread crumbs, eggs, mint, water, and salt and pepper. Using your hands, squeeze the mixture between your fingers making sure it is well combined.

2. Using 2 tbsp/30g of mixture for each meatball, shape into balls, toss in a little flour, shaking off the excess. Flatten each ball slightly into the palm of your hand.

3. Heat* the oil in a pan and cook each meatball for approximately three minutes (each side) until they are a dark brown colour and cooked through.

4. Drain on absorbent paper.

5. Serve hot or cold with fresh tomato relish (see next page).

Note:

To test the oil for frying, toss a little flour into the oil: when it sizzles, the oil is ready for frying.

The meatballs should be flattened out before cooking as they will puff up and rise whilst cooking.

Meatballs (Keftedes)

Ingredients

2 cups13oz/375g brown onions, finely chopped

2½ lb/1kg lean ground beef

½ cup/4oz/125g dry bread crumbs

2 eggs

1 tbsp/15g chopped mint

4 tbsp/2fl oz/50 ml water

salt and freshly ground black pepper

2 cups/16fl oz/500ml vegetable oil, for frying

Method

1. Place chicken mince in a bowl, grate the onion into the ground beef, and add remaining ingredients. Mix well to combine, and knead a little by hand. With wet hands roll into balls. Heat oil ½in/1cm deep in a frying pan, and sauté the rissoles on both sides until they turn color. Remove to a plate.

2. To the pan add the onion and garlic, and sauté until transparent. Add remaining sauce ingredients, and bring to the boil. Return rissoles to the pan, reduce heat, cover and simmer for 30 minutes.

3. Serve over boiled spaghetti or Greek pasta, if preferred.

Ingredients

Rissoles:

2 cups/1lb/500g ground chicken meat

1 medium onion, grated

2 tbsp/30g parsley, minced

½ tsp/2.5g salt

pepper

1 egg

½ cup/4oz/125g breadcrumbs, dried

1 tbsp/15ml water

oil for frying

Greek style chicken rissoles
in tomato sauce

Tomato Sauce:

1 medium onion, minced

1 clove garlic, crushed

1 tbsp/15ml oil

1¾ cups/14oz/440g canned tomatoes

1 tbsp/15ml tomato paste

½ cup/4fl oz/125ml water

½ tsp/2.5g oregano, dried

1 tsp/5g sugar

salt, pepper

1 tbsp/15g minced parsley

Method

1. Peel away membrane from liver, and cut out tubes and any green sections. Cut into thin slices, place in a large dish, pour milk over liver, and leave to soak for one hour.

2. Heat oil in a large saucepan. Add garlic, onion, and bacon, and cook for 2-3 minutes. Set aside in a dish.

3. Heat extra oil in the same saucepan, dip liver in seasoned flour, and cook quickly on both sides. Set aside and keep warm. Return onion and bacon to pan, add parsley, oregano, lemon juice, salt, and pepper, and heat through.

4. Pour mixture over liver and serve.

Ingredients

1½lb/750g lamb's liver

½ cup/4fl oz/125ml milk

1 tbsp/15ml olive oil

1 clove garlic, crushed

1 medium red onion, sliced

8 oz/250g bacon, cut into strips

Lamb's liver with lemon and oregano

¼ cup/2fl oz/60ml olive oil, extra

⅓ cup/3oz/85g flour, seasoned

1 tbsp/15g parsley, chopped

1 tsp/5g oregano, chopped

¼ cup/2fl oz/60ml lemon juice

salt and freshly ground pepper

greek

Method

1. Combine lemon juice, olive, oil, garlic, lemon thyme, and salt and pepper in a bowl, and marinate the lamb for at least 1-2 hours, or overnight.

2. Combine all salad ingredients in a bowl and set aside.

3. Mix all the ingredients for the yogurt sauce together in a bowl, and set aside.

4. Broil or barbecue the lamb pieces for a few minutes each side until lamb is cooked, but still slightly pink in the center. Fill each pita bread with the lamb, salad and yogurt sauce, and serve warm.

Ingredients

½ cup/2fl oz/60ml lemon juice

5 tbsp/2½fl oz/80ml olive oil

1 clove garlic, crushed

1 tsp/5g lemon thyme, chopped

salt and pepper

11oz/350g lean lamb, cubed

4 small pita breads

Salad:

1 small cucumber, cubed

2 beefsteak tomatoes, quartered

1 Bermuda onion, sliced

¼ cup/2oz/60g feta cheese, crumbled

2 tbsp/30ml olive oil

Marinated lamb kebabs with pita, salad and yogurt sauce (Arni Souvlakia)

1 tbsp/15ml vinegar

salt and pepper

Yogurt Sauce:

1 scant cup/7 fl oz/200g plain yogurt

1 clove garlic, crushed

⅓ cup/3oz/100g grated cucumber

1 tsp/5g chopped mint

salt and pepper to taste

Method

1. Cut each pouch along one side. With a sharp knife, score inside skin diagonally in both directions. Cut calamari into rectangles, each 1x1½in/2 x 4cm.

2. In a bowl, combine the farina (semolina), salt and pepper.

3. Heat oil in a large frying pan or wok. Dip calamari into farina (semolina) and, when oil is hot, cook a few at a time (until lightly brown and crisp). Drain on absorbent paper and serve with lemon wedges.

Ingredients

1½lb/700g calamari pouches

½ cup fine farina (semolina)

1 tsp/5g salt

1 tsp/5g ground pepper

½ cup/4fl oz/250ml olive oil, for frying

1 lemon, cut into wedges

Pan fried calamari with lemon
(Kalamaria Tiganita)

Method

1. Heat 1 tbsp/15ml oil in a large frying pan.

2. Add pork and brown quickly for 2-3 minutes each side. Set meat aside.

3. Heat extra oil in pan. Add garlic and onion, and cook for 2-3 minutes. Add quince and cook for a further three minutes. Add white wine and cook for two minutes (or until reduced).

4. Stir in orange juice, chicken broth, cinnamon stick, and honey, cook on a low heat for 10-15 minutes (or until sauce has thickened slightly). Return meat to pan, and cook for a further 5-10 minutes. Stir in parsley, salt and pepper, spoon over cutlets, and serve.

Ingredients

1 tbsp/15ml olive oil

4 pork cutlets

Sauce:

4 tsp/20ml olive oil

1 clove garlic, crushed

1 medium red onion, sliced

1 medium quince, peeled, cored, and cut into thin slices

Pork cutlets with quince

½ cup/4fl oz/125ml white wine

juice of 1 orange (around ⅓ cup/2½fl oz/80ml)

½ cup/4fl oz/125ml chicken broth

cinnamon stick

1 tbsp/15ml honey

1 tbsp/15g parsley, chopped

salt and freshly ground pepper

greek

Method

1. Heat the oil in a large saucepan and sauté the onion and garlic over a low heat, until transparent. Add tomatoes, sugar, salt, and pepper.

2. Simmer gently for 20 minutes. Add the basil, and keep warm.

3. Pre-heat broiler or barbecue grill to moderate

4. Cut swordfish, green bell pepper, and eggplant (aubergine) into large cubes.

5. Arrange on eight skewers, alternating with the rosemary sprigs. Brush with olive oil and chopped rosemary.

6. Broil or grill kabobs, turning over at least once to brown the sides. Baste with a little more sauce. The swordfish should be golden, with the herbs and vegetables slightly charred.

7. Serve with extra sauce.

Swordfish kebabs with tomato sauce

Ingredients

1 tbsp/15ml olive oil

1 small onion, finely diced

2 cloves garlic, crushed

2 x 13oz/400g cans tomatoes, drained

½ tsp/2.5g sugar

½ tsp/2.5g salt

½ tsp/2.5g pepper

1½lb/750g swordfish

1 green bell pepper, deseeded

1 medium eggplant (aubergine)

6 sprigs rosemary

3 tbsp/1½fl oz/40ml olive oil

1 tbsp/15g chopped rosemary

salt and freshly ground black pepper

Method

1. Heat the oil and sauté the onion for five minutes. Add the ground meat and cook for ten minutes, breaking it up with a fork as it cooks.

2. Add the tomato paste, tomatoes, water, oregano, sugar, Worcestershire sauce, and the cinnamon stick and bring to the boil, then simmer for 45 minutes (until mixture is cooked and sauce is thick). Add more water during cooking if needed. Season with salt and pepper.

3. To make the béchamel sauce, melt the butter in a saucepan, add the flour, and cook for three minutes. Add the milk, and, stirring continuously, bring to the boil, then simmer until sauce thickens to a good coating consistency. Add the cheese and four egg yolks to the sauce, mixing well, then season with salt and pepper.

4. In a large ovenproof dish, mix the penne and the ground meat together, and add two eggs to the mixture. Pour the béchamel sauce over the top, sprinkle with the additional cheese, and bake in the oven for 30-45 minutes, until top is golden brown and the pastitzio is set.

5. Slice and serve hot or cold with a Greek salad.

Ingredients

4 tbsp/2fl oz/60ml oil

1 onion, sliced

2½lb/1kg lean ground beef

2 tbsp/30ml tomato paste

13oz/400g can tomatoes

1 cup/8fl oz/250ml water

2 tsp/10g chopped oregano

1 tsp/5g sugar

1 tbsp/15ml Worcestershire sauce

1 cinnamon stick

Pastitzio (Greek Lasagna)

salt and pepper

1¾ cups/13oz/400g penne, cooked

2 whole eggs

¾ cup/6oz/175g grated Romano cheese, for the
topping

Béchamel Sauce:

½ cup/4oz/125g unsalted butter

6 tbsp/45g flour

4 cups/1¾ pints/1 l milk

1 cup/8oz/250g Romano cheese

4 egg yolks

Method

In a food processor, combine the nuts, and cookies until finely ground.

Add the baking powder and lemon zest, and pulse briefly.

Beat the egg whites with the cream of tartar until soft peaks form, then continue beating while adding 4 tbsp/60g sugar, one at a time. Once the sugar has been added and dissolved, the whites should be stiff and glossy.

In a clean bowl, beat together the egg yolks and remaining sugar until the mixture is thick and pale.

Fold the nut mixture into the yolks, then add the melted butter and stir thoroughly to combine. Preheat the oven to 350°F/180°C.

Pour the cake batter on top of the whites and gently fold it in, using a spatula.

Spoon the cake batter into a greased and floured 12x8in/30cm x 20cm cake pan or metal baking dish then sprinkle the remaining nuts over the top.

Bake for 40 minutes or until set in the center.

Meanwhile, make the rum syrup. Bring the sugar and water to the boil and simmer for five minutes. Add the rum and continue boiling for three more minutes then set aside to cool.

When the cake is ready, remove it from the oven and pour the warm syrup over it.

Allow to cool then cut into diamond shapes, like baklava. Serve with a little extra syrup drizzled over it.

Greek rum and hazelnut cake

Ingredients

For the Cake:

500g toasted hazelnuts

⅔ cup/3½ oz/100g vanilla cookies, crushed

2 tsp/10g baking powder

1 lemon, rind grated

8 large eggs, separated

¼ tsp/1.25g cream of tartar

1 cup/250g/8 oz sugar

⅔ cup/4½oz/135g butter, melted

⅔ cup/4½oz/100g toasted hazelnuts or almonds, coarsely chopped

For the Syrup:

1 cup/250g/8 oz sugar

½ cup/4fl oz/125ml water

⅓ cup/4fl oz/100ml dark rum

Note:

The easiest way to cut a rectangular cake into diamonds is as follows:
First, cut three or four strips of cake from one end of the pan to the
other. Then, hold the knife at a 45-degree angle and cut further strips
diagonally across the pan.

Method

1. Pre-heat oven to 350°F/180°C.

2. Grease an 8in/20cm cake pan, and line with paper.

3. In a large bowl, combine butter, sugar, and rind. Using an electric beater, cream butter, sugar, and rind until light and fluffy.

4. Add the eggs, one at a time, beating well after each addition.

5. Fold in semolina, baking powder, and ground almonds. Add raisins, almonds, and yogurt, and lightly fold in.

6. Pour mixture into prepared cake pan and bake for 35-45 minutes (or until cake is lightly browned on top).

7. To make the syrup, combine sugar, lemon juice, and honey in a small saucepan. Cook on a low heat for 15-20 minutes, or the liquid thickens into a syrup.

8. Using a metal skewer, poke holes in the cake at regular intervals. Cool syrup slightly, then pour it over the cake so that it absorbs the syrup. Serve with whipped cream.

Ingredients

½ cup/4oz/125g butter, softened

¾ cup/6oz/175g caster (superfine) sugar

1 lemon, rind finely grated

4 eggs

1 cup/8oz/250g fine farina (semolina, cream of wheat)

2 tsp/10g baking powder

1 cup/8oz/250g ground almonds

Lemon and yogurt semolina **cake**

1 cup/8oz/250g raisins

½ cup/4oz/125g flaked almonds

1 scant cup/7oz/200g yogurt

Syrup:

1 cup/8oz/250g superfine (caster) sugar

½ cup/4fl oz/250ml lemon juice

½ cup/4fl oz/250ml honey

1 cup/8 fl oz/250ml whipping cream, to serve

greek

Method

1. Pre-heat oven to 350°F/180°C.

2. Peel and slice the apples thinly. Place in a greased, shallow ovenproof dish.

Stir in the dates, lemon and orange juices, rind, and cinnamon sticks.

Drizzle the honey over the mixture.

3. Cover and bake for 45–55 minutes, until tender and flavors are absorbed.

4. Serve warm or chilled dusted with cinnamon. Serve Greek yogurt on the side.

Baked fresh dates and apples

Ingredients

5 large tart apples

butter, for greasing

1 scant cup/7oz/200g dates, pitted and halved

1/2 lemon, juice squeezed

2 oranges, juice squeezed, 1 rind finely grated

2 cinnamon sticks

3 tbsp/45ml clear honey

ground cinnamon, to garnish

about 1 cup/250ml/8 fl oz yogurt, to serve

Method

1. Pre-heat the oven to 340°F/170°C.

2. Beat the butter with the sugar until pale and creamy, then add the vanilla and almonds, and mix thoroughly. Add the egg yolk and mix until well combined. Sift the flour, and fold it into the mixture with a metal spoon.
Bring the dough together with your hands, and knead lightly for two minutes, until smooth. Wrap in plastic wrap and refrigerate for 15 minutes.

3. Flatten out the dough with your hands to a thickness of ½-¾in/1-2cm, and roll into crescent shapes. Place a clove in the center of each cookie, and bake on a cookie sheet for 15 minutes, or until cookies are golden.

4. Remove from the oven, place on a sheet of nonstick baking paper and, while still hot, sift powdered sugar thickly over the cookies. Let them cool, and store in an airtight container.

Almond shortbread **cookies**

Ingredients

1¾ cups/14 oz /400g butter, clarified

2 tbsp/50g superfine (caster) sugar

1 tbsp/15ml vanilla extract

⅔ cup/3½ oz/100g roasted blanched almonds

1 egg yolk

2 cups/700g all-purpose (plain) flour

cloves

about 1 cup/125g/125g powdered sugar

Method

Grease a 10in/24cm square or round cake pan generously and coat with some of the shredded coconut. Preheat the oven to 375°F/190°C.

Sift together the plain flour and baking powder.

Cream the butter and sugar until light and fluffy. With the motor of the electric beater running, add the eggs one at a time and beat well after each addition.

Fold in the olive oil, coconut, toasted shredded coconut, figs, and flour mixture and combine thoroughly.

Pour into the prepared tin and bake at for 10 minutes, then reduce the heat to 300°F/150°C and bake for a further 65 minutes or until "springy" when pressed gently on the surface.

Meanwhile, slice off the thin yellow rind of the lemons and slice into strips.

Boil the sugar, lemon rind strips, and lemon juice for 3 minutes and strain, reserving the strips for garnish.

When the cake has been removed from the oven, pour the syrup over the cake and allow the cake to cool.

Gently run a knife between the cake and the pan and remove the cake.

Slice and serve, garnished with the caramelized strips of lemon rind.

Ingredients

For the Cake:

3 cups/1 lb/450g shredded unsweetened coconut

2 cups/8oz/250g all-purpose (plain) flour

4 tsp/20g baking powder

1 scant cup/7oz/200g butter

2 cups/1 lb/450g superfine (caster) sugar

7 large eggs

Greek coconut and fig cake

2 tbsp/50ml light olive oil

1 cup/8 oz/250g toasted sweetened shredded coconut

⅓ cup/3oz/80g dried mission figs, chopped

For the syrup:

1½ cups/12oz/350g sugar

3 lemons, rind peeled juice squeezed

greek

Method

1. Melt butter, set aside.

2. Mix the nuts in a bowl with the cinnamon and sugar.

3. Brush a 10x14in/25x33cm cookie sheet with the butter.

4. Line the cookie sheet with one sheet of filo with ends hanging over the sides. Brush the dough melted butter and add another layer of filo. Repeat with 8 more filo sheets.

5. Sprinkle the nut mixture generously over the filo. Continue the layering of filo pastry, using 3 sheets of filo to one layer of nuts, brushing each filo sheet with melted butter, until all nuts are used up. Preheat the oven to 450°F/230°C.

6. Top with 8 reserved sheets of filo, making sure the top sheet is well buttered. Score the top lengthwise in parallel strips.

7. Bake for 30 minutes, then reduce heat to 300°F/150°C and bake for a further hour. Pour cold syrup over baklava and cut into diamond shapes.

8. **Syrup:** Place ingredients in saucepan and bring to the boil. Reduce heat and let simmer for 10-15 minutes. Leave to cool before use.

Baklava

Ingredients

1 cup/8oz/250g unsalted butter, melted

13oz/400g almonds, blanched, toasted and ground

1½tsp/7.5 g cinnamon

½ cup/4oz/125g superfine (caster) sugar

1 lb 8oz/700g filo dough

Syrup:

3 cups/1 lb 8 oz/700g Superfine (caster) sugar

1½ cups/12 fl oz/350ml water

1 cinnamon stick

1 piece of orange or lemon rind

1 tbsp/15ml honey

Almond cakes 54

Almond shortbread cookies 90

Artichokes la polita 30

Baby octopus marinated in olive oil
and oregano 40

Baby spinach, feta, artichokes
and walnut salad 8

Baked fish 38

Baked fresh dates and apples 88

Baked sardine fillets 26

Baklava 94

Beef with artichokes, olive and oregano 34

Lime beans with broiled haloumi
and lemon 46

Deep fried okra 66

Dips 12

Eggplant rolls 44

Fennel and zucchini cakes 60

Feta and ricotta stuffed tomatoes 14

Greek coconut and fig cake 92

Greek orzo salad with olives
and bell peppers 20

Greek rum and hazelnut cake 84

Greek salad 6

Greek style chicken rissoles
in tomato sauce 70

Broiled goat's cheese salad 18

Chicken kebabs with yogurt
and lemon sauce 58

Chicken with oregano and lemon 56

Chicken, roasted bell pepper,
olives, & feta pie 32

Chickpea, roasted tomato, and garlic soup 10

Chilled yogurt soup 16

Lamb shanks with lima (broad) beans,
olives, & risoni 62

Lamb's liver with lemon and oregano 72

Lemon and yogurt semolina cake 86

Marinated lamb kebabs with pita,
salad, and yogurt 74

Meatballs (keftedes) 68

Meatballs in egg and lemon soup 22

Mixed bean and vegetable soup 24

Pan fried calamari with lemon 76

Pastitzio 82

Pork cutlets with quince 78

Rice with chicken livers,
pine nuts, and currants 50

Roasted red bell pepper with feta,
eggplant, olives, and sun-dried tomatoes 36

Salmon and feta filo packages 42

Sardines and broiled peppers 28

Cornish hens (poussin) in vine leaves 52

Spinach, olive and feta frittata
with roasted bell pepper sauce 48

Swordfish kebabs with tomato sauce 80

Zucchini and feta pie 64

Index